Go

for All

The InterAct Series

GEORGE W. RENWICK, Series Editor

A Fair Go for All

Australian/American Interactions

GEORGE W. RENWICK
Revised by
Reginald Smart and
Don L. Henderson

INTERCULTURAL PRESS, INC.

For information, contact:
Intercultural Press, Inc.
P.O. Box 700
Yarmouth, Maine 04096, USA

© 1991 by George W. Renwick

Printer in the United States of America.

97 96 95 94 93 92   2 3 4 5 6 7

Library of Congress Cataloging-in-Publication Data

Renwick, George W.
    A fair go for all: a guide for Australians and Americans/George Renwick: revised by Reginald Smart and Don L. Henderson.
      p. cm.—(InterAct series)
    ISBN 0-933662-96-3
    1. United States—Relations—Australia. 2. Australia—Relations—United States. 3. National characteristics, American.
4. National characteristics, Australian. 5. United States—Social life and customs—20th century. 6. Australia—Social life and customs. 7. Intercultural communication—United States. 8. Intercultural communication—Australia. I. Smart, Reginald George, 1936- II. Henderson, Don L. III. Title. IV. Series.
E183.8.A8R46 1991
303.48'273094—dc20
                               91-9628
                                CIP

Contents

Preface

This was the first book in a series—the *InterAct Series*—which examines the interactions between Americans and people from other countries and cultures. We are pleased, therefore, to publish a revision of the work that launched this series.

A cultural interaction study like this one probes, explains, and predicts what happens when individuals who have grown up in contrasting cultures meet, eat, joke, argue, negotiate, and work with one another. Such a study makes clear what each person must do in order to become a clever competitor, a valued coworker or a trusted colleague and friend.

This volume and other volumes in the InterAct Series explain how people from one culture see those in another, what exactly they expect from each other, how they affect each other when they are together, and how what is said by one embarrasses, frustrates, motivates, impresses, or angers the other.

The authors of this InterAct are uniquely qualified to explore Australian and American cultures and how the people from each relate to each other.

George Renwick wrote the original version at the request of a major U.S. multinational corporation with operations in Australia. The company had been experiencing friction between its Australian and American employees and hired Mr. Renwick in a consulting and training role to help them ameliorate the problem. When published, the book was well received in both the U.S. and Australia where it was excerpted in the Australian press.

Mr. Renwick is president of Renwick and Associates, a consulting firm which provides cross-cultural research, consulting, and training services to international companies. He first worked with Australians in Hong Kong in 1963. Since then he has worked with Australian managers in multinational firms in other Asian countries as well as in the United States. Mr. Renwick spends a great deal of his time working with business personnel on site in countries around the world. He is also a visiting professor at the American Graduate School of International Management (Thunderbird) in Glendale, Arizona.

In revising the original edition of the work, the Intercultural Press sought assistance from two Australians with extensive experience working in the U.S. with Americans.

Dr. Reginald Smart is currently a professor of speech communication at California State University at Long Beach. He has been a private cross-cultural consultant to international business and nonprofit organizations in the U S. and Australia since 1976 and from 1979 to 1983 was Lead Trainer, Australian Institute of Management, Sydney, Australia. He has published a number of books and articles on international education, cross-cultural training, and intercultural communication.

The other revisions editor, Don L. Henderson, contributes the perspective of an Australian who has worked for many years in American organizations. He is currently working on Wall Street with the training department of a major financial institution. Much of his career has been devoted to the cross-cultural aspects of sales and management training in the financial industry. In this capacity, he has conducted numerous training programs around the world. Henderson is also an adjunct professor at N.Y.U. School of Continuing Education, where he teaches a course in cross-cultural strategies for international business.

We are confident that the readers of this InterAct will find it a helpful resource in understanding the contrasts and similari-

ties of Australian and American cultures and in seeking more
enjoyable and productive relationships with people from the
other culture whom they encounter.

David S. Hoopes
Editor-in-Chief

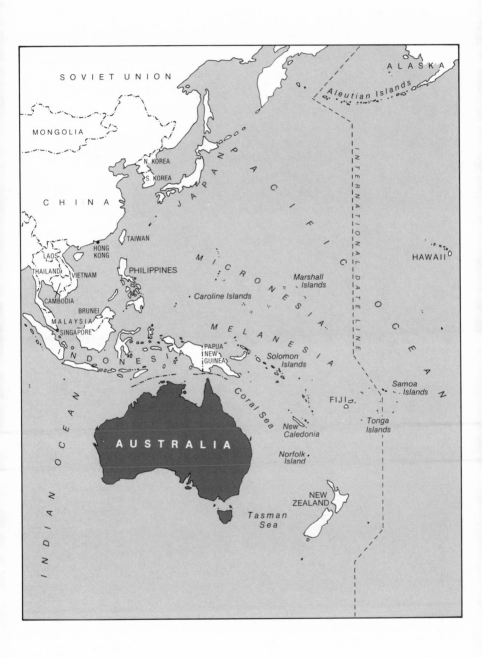

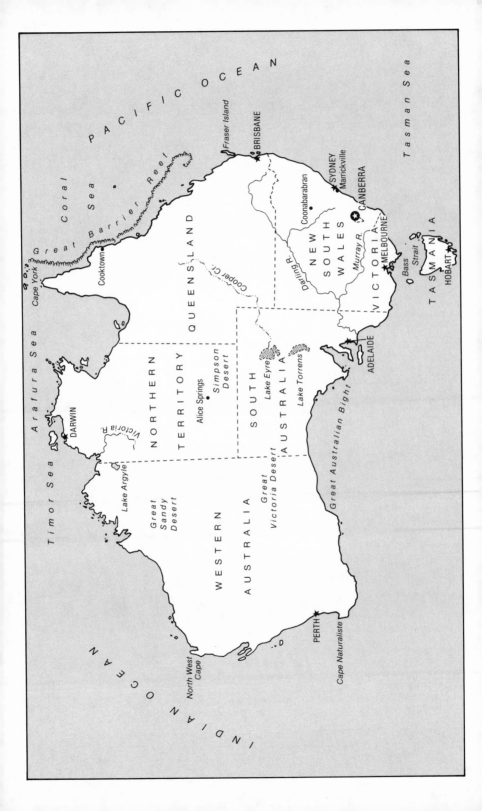

Introduction

Australians and Americans have usually had rather high regard for one another—as long as they were some distance apart. It would seem these two peoples should be able to get along well together. Frequently, however, they do not. Australians and Americans expect a great deal of one another, but their expectations are often frustrated. Many are surprised by the underlying tension that sometimes develops between them and by the subsequent ambivalence in their feelings about one another. Thus, conflicts can, and do, occur, but the cultural causes are often subtle, and the individuals frequently unable to articulate or identify them.

There are several reasons why Australians and Americans experience difficulties in their personal relationships:

1. They have many similarities, thus their differences tend to stand out and become especially annoying.

2. What determines the level of tension and conflict between two peoples is not on how *many* points they differ, but on *which* points. If the points on which they differ are not important to either, there will be little conflict. However, if the points of greatest contrast, even though few, are particularly significant to each, conflict is more likely to result, and Americans and Australians do differ on such points.

1

3. Perhaps most importantly, when two peoples *expect* to encounter differences in one another (as, for example, do Americans and the Japanese), their discovery of a similarity is exciting and reassuring. But when each expects the other to be much like themselves (as Australians and Americans do) and then encounter a difference, they are taken aback and confused. And the more differences they encounter, the more irritated they become, especially when the dissimilarities are so subtle that they escape being consciously identified and dealt with.

The source of the differences between Australians and Americans can, of course, be traced to the distinctive cultures in which they have grown up and which have imparted to them distinctive ways of thinking and behaving. The result is a set of general characteristics shared by most, though not all, members of the two cultures. In looking at cultures from this perspective we are aware that we will be dealing in generalizations which are not wholly true for any particular individual. Cultures, however, do have characteristics that are predominant, that is, that are shared by the large majority of their members and which make them unique. It will be useful here to examine the predominant cultural characteristics of Australians and Americans and then use these as a framework for better understanding how the differences between the two affect their interaction. We will then also be able to suggest specific ways in which Americans and Australians can deal with each other so as to foster more successful relationships.

In this study we will analyze the two cultures, identify important points of similarity and difference, describe how these are manifested in individual Australians and Americans, explore particular difficulties that arise between them, and recommend ways in which their interaction can be made more rewarding. We will also examine the interaction process itself, that is, the direct effect Americans and Australians have on one another.

The behavior of people in a personal relationship follows not only from the interplay of their differing backgrounds and distinctive cultural characteristics, but is affected also by the specific nature of their relationship. An American, for instance, may think, feel, and do things with an Australian that he or she probably would not with someone, say, from Japan. Interaction with an Australian may generate perceptions and evoke responses which interaction with a person from some other culture would not. More specifically, Australians and Americans often evoke in each other exactly that behavior which reinforces their preconceptions. These preconceptions are sometimes not very complimentary and become even less so as the interaction progresses. In this study, therefore, we will suggest specific things Americans and Australians can do (and specific things they should *not* do) to further the development of more positive mutual perceptions and reactions.

The accuracy of the perceptions which Australians and Americans have of each other is critical. If these impressions are correct, the interaction will be more productive, or at least, constructive. If the impressions are incorrect, misunderstandings will leave people feeling ineffective, frustrated, and annoyed if not angry. Americans, for instance, tend to see Australians as self-satisfied and arrogant. Australians often consider Americans to be boastful and superficial, what Australians call "all show and no substance." These mutual perceptions, or misperceptions, can be quite negative and distressing to people who generally think of each other as "good friends."

In light of the above, the first question (from the American perspective) is: "What are Australians like? What are their characteristic patterns of thinking and behaving, and what expectations do they bring to an interpersonal encounter?" The next and equally important question is, "What do Australians feel and how do they behave when they are with Americans in America?" Australians, of course, should make corresponding inquiries of Americans. This book will explore the implications of these and a final question: "What should Americans or Australians do when they know the answers to the first two questions?"

In this exploration we will focus on the customary behavior, patterns of thinking, and styles of communication of individual

Americans and Australians. We will not, however, devote much attention to the institutions of culture: governmental or organizational structures, religion, artistic and literary production, or educational systems. Further, since there is currently little research available on how nonverbal communication (gestures, intonation, the use of space, etc.) affects Australian-American interaction, we shall not devote much attention to that subject either.

Obviously, basic cultural characteristics described herein are not found in every Australian or every American. Certainly, they are not found to the same degree in each person. What we are suggesting is (1) that some American cultural characteristics are shared by large numbers of Americans and some Australian cultural characteristics are shared by large numbers of Australians and (2) that these characteristics often affect interactions between people from the two countries.

In the course of our study we will discuss the perceptions which Australians and Americans have of each other. We believe it will be useful to describe these mutual perceptions, which are sometimes quite negative, but the descriptions should not be taken as an indictment of either people. They are presented simply to enable us to analyze more effectively cross-cultural interaction between people who, in the abstract, think of each other as "good friends."

It is our hope that with a better understanding of how and why they differ and of the impact these differences have on their personal relationships, Australians and Americans will be able to deal more effectively with their negative perceptions and be able to respond more productively when they encounter each other socially and professionally.

2

Similarities

Australia and the United States are nations of immigrants; their ideas and institutions, along with their people, were transplanted from Great Britain. Because of their common heritage, a majority of Australians and Americans speak the same language, follow the Christian religion, and believe in social and political democracy. There are strong similarities as well in the ways they behave—in their way of greeting people and in their customs of eating, drinking, and dressing.

Conscious of the fact that their cultures are derivative, Australians and Americans have encouraged the development of distinctive national identities, especially admiring individuals who assert their freedom from the traditions of their forebears. Similarly, they are antagonistic toward authority, especially when it is exercised by a distant "them." As pioneer peoples, they have stressed the practical and innovative. Both have been ready to break with the past and discard the transplanted ideas and institutions which have failed to survive in the new environment. Both place relatively low value on intellectual and spiritual pursuits. They prefer, for example, not to discuss world politics and philosophical or ethical issues, and when they do, they rarely discuss them with any degree of academic sophistication. They are adaptable, direct, and forthright. Further, they are considered very informal in speech and manner, both using first names quickly, for example, regardless of who the person is or what the degree of intimacy is.

Not surprisingly, most people in these two countries assume that their own beliefs and ways of doing things are better than the available alternatives. Any challenge to such assumptions is not regarded kindly, perhaps the more so because both countries, after their initial settlement, existed for a long time in comparative isolation.

Like most Americans, Australians are very mobile, albeit in different ways. Americans migrate freely and frequently from state to state, whereas the Australians are insatiable world travelers. Both seem to invest less in *place* than their European counterparts, though Australians are much more likely than Americans to live all their lives in the city or town in which they were born.

Americans and Australians are now accustomed to living in highly industrialized and thoroughly urban environments. Both are proud of being modern. Most Australians living in the United States and most Americans living in Australia find the environment familiar, about what they expected it to be. There may be contrasts, such as Sydney's ubiquitous houses of red brick with red-tiled roofs separated by high wooden fences compared with the American single homes, duplexes, and condos built of wood, stone, or brick, standing side by side without fences. But the basic intent is similar: both want family-owned homes in and around which they can express their individuality without restriction. This kind of individualism ranks near the top in the hierarchy of values in these two cultures.

They both live a high-consumption lifestyle, seeing in *things* the means to "the good life" and relegating the life of the mind and spirit to a somewhat lower place. Both love automobiles and value the independence owning a car permits.

Given a common heritage, a similar pioneering experience, and resulting similar personal characteristics, Australians and Americans usually assume that they understand each other more than they actually do. In reality, there are important differences—differences in values, priorities, attitudes, motivations, and ways of interacting—which have a profound effect on relationships between them. These differences will be examined in detail in the pages which follow.

3

Differences

The Land

Australia and the United States are approximately the same size. But while one contains the richest soil on earth coupled with rainfall adequate for growing enough crops to feed half the world, the other is primarily desert with a watered rim. Australia was inhospitable, was settled by Europeans much later than America, and was never the site of a war for independence. England sent convicts to the free colonies in North America for only a short time, while Australia was settled primarily to accommodate those social castoffs of England and Ireland which the Americans, after independence, no longer accepted. (Hence the proximity of American independence in 1776 to Sydney's settlement in 1788.) America's initial colonists voluntarily settled a land of verdant forests and rolling hills, searching for a place to freely practice their religion and, particularly in the south, pursue mercantile ventures. In contrast, the first Australians were involuntarily thrown together—convicts and their soldier-jailers—and deposited on a sandstone shore walled off by dense and thorny bush. American ideas and attitudes were strongly influenced by the relatively intense religious beliefs brought to the New World by the Puritans, the Quakers, the Scotch-Irish, and other groups.

Religious intensity did not characterize those who went to Australia, and the difference in religious outlook remains a major contrast between the two nations.

It is true that the optimistic settlers and prospectors who were soon streaming to nineteenth-century Australia shared a frontier spirit similar to that of the immigrants to the United States. Nevertheless, the fundamental differences in the origins of the settlers and in the land they encountered led to the development of their respective cultures in markedly different directions.

Until as late as the mid-1960s, Australians were overwhelmingly British and Irish. The United States, on the other hand, had long welcomed immigrants from every part of Europe, had imported massive numbers of Africans as slaves, and had absorbed large populations from China, Japan, and Mexico as well as the whole French territory of Louisiana. Immigrants to America also encountered Native Americans, who occupied the land and who played a much larger part in shaping the society than the aborigines (the Koori people, as they are now called) did in Australia. The result of these differences was homogeneity and a strong sense of isolation and exclusivity in Australia and heterogeneity in the U.S. Though they developed an isolationist foreign policy, Americans gradually overcame their feelings of isolation from Europe. And they rejected exclusivity on principle. The melting pot could make anyone an "American"—at least so it was believed until doubts arose in the midtwentieth century.

While the land of Australia was forbidding, nurturing little but acerbic toughness, North America offered endless riches, fostering optimism. The gentle leafage and soft carpets of pine needles of a New England forest contrasted strikingly with the harsh Australian bush, with its predominance of prickles and spines. For the Australians with the courage to venture beyond the coastal rim, travel brought more of the same, but drier, while in the U.S., the interior revealed incredible variety and wealth. Harshness marked the one, fecundity the other. The one produced a brash, taciturn friendliness, the other an optimistic, idealistic pragmatism.

It would be difficult to truly appreciate cultural differences between these two nations if one didn't grasp the significance of the land in the development of its peoples. The Australian view is captured in the words of the popular contemporary artist, Mandy Martin, who explains that the Australian landscape "dominates the culture."[1] And nothing better demonstrates the Australian psychological attachment to the land than the second and last verses of the poem "My Country" by Dorothea Mackellar (1885-1968). These verses can be recited by every ten-year-old Australian in much the same way that "America the Beautiful" is sung by an American child.

I love a sunburnt country,
A land of sweeping plains,
Of ragged mountain ranges,
Of droughts and flooding rains.
I love her fair horizons,
I love her jewel-sea,
Her beauty and her terror—
The wide brown land for me!

An opal-hearted country,
A willful, lavish land—
All you who have not loved her,
You will not understand—
Though Earth holds many splendours,
Wherever I may die,
I know to what brown country
My homing thoughts will fly.

Today, Australians see real life focused in a handful of oases, seven sizable state capital cities and, to a much lesser extent, a score of much smaller towns. Almost all centers of population are found within fifty miles of the coast and contain over 90 percent of the population. These coastal dwellers rarely venture inland. The "myth of the bush" depicted in the film *Crocodile Dundee*, that is, Australia as a nation of rugged outback fron-

12

tiersmen able to survive easily in a hostile environment, is just that—a myth—though it still enchants Australians, much as the myth of the Wild West captivates many Americans. The population of Australia is only one-fifteenth that of the U.S. (16.5 million vs. 240 million), but it is spread over a geographic area roughly the same size. The result is a different sense of space and vulnerability—the "great Australian loneliness," it is called. If you are not in one of the seven urban enclaves, you aren't really anywhere in Australia.

Australians build their cities out rather than up. The tallest building in Newcastle, Australia's sixth largest city, for example, is only ten stories (eleven by U.S. count). Any comparable American city would have many taller structures. This difference in the way Australians and Americans react to space can also be observed in the claustrophobic responses many Australians have to a place like Manhattan and other large American cities. Conversely, the American view is reflected in the comments of visitors to cities other than Australia's two large metropolises, Sydney and Melbourne. "These are more like towns than cities," they will say, and, of course, to the Americans they are. But this different sense of space is obviously not only reflected in the way Australians and Americans build cities. For example, in 1978 former U.S. Senator Eugene McCarthy, on a brief visit to Australia, noted that the people were more confined by distance than by walls. The problem with Australia, he said, "is not so much one of time (an American value) as it is one of space. Australians, as a rule, do not say it will take too long to get somewhere—they say it is too far." Such differences are embedded in the cultural fabric.

Social Structure

Given the contrasts in geography, origin of immigrants, and settlement patterns, it is not surprising that differences between Australians and Americans are also found in the way their societies are structured.

A number of myths influence Australian thinking. In addition to the myth of the bush, another is the "myth of the worker." Australians can boast of having one of the first militant trade union movements in the world, and during the first half of the twentieth century there was a strong tendency among large numbers of Australians to identify themselves with the working class. But this myth has gone the way of the myth of the bush. Both are vestiges of the past and have little force among contemporary Australians, who would rather have the Australian entrepreneur Rupert Murdoch's millions than be a "cockey" (farmer) or a "wharfie" (longshoreman). Only a small number of Australians, for instance, work the land (even though three-quarters of Australia's exports are derived from it), and the nation's largest social grouping is the white-collar worker. More than half of the population describe themselves as middle-class. You'll search the Australian pub scene for a long time to find a true Crocodile Dundee.

The "myth of egalitarianism," on the other hand, carries more weight. In spite of real class divisions, this myth retains the power to modify the way Aussies treat each other, at least superficially. Thus, the boss always goes about the office or plant in shirtsleeves and accepts being called "mate." Federal cabinet ministers travel in the front seat of their limos in much the same way that a taxi driver expects a single passenger to ride in the front seat. This can be disconcerting to Americans who, when they get in the back seat of a taxi, are likely to hear, "What's wrong? You got leprosy?" Even proper grammar can bring a quietly muttered, "Who the hell does he think he is?"

But scratch the surface in the Land Down Under and you'll find clear class demarcations. When they leave their Sydney offices, the bosses travel north, the others mostly south. Front-office people avoid visiting the factory floor if at all possible. And to aspiring white-collar workers the suburb one resides in is as important as driving one's car to work (rather than using the perfectly adequate public transportation system). A careful look at top management will reveal very few who have attended the free, state-run high schools; everyone knows you have to go to a private school "if you want to get anywhere." And among those schools there is a clearly defined pecking order, headed by the top private school, Geelong Grammar.

At the top, then, are a very small number of people educated in private schools and possessing for the most part "old" money. This group tends to come from the land, the "squatters" as they are called, and from certain industries such as the media and investment or merchant banking. It is a difficult group for an outsider to break into, but squatters are accorded little special regard because of their status. As the Australian joke goes: "A squatter is nothing more than a farmer who drives a Rolls Royce—with a roll of barbed wire and three ewe lambs in the back seat!" Australians resist recognizing class differences, and when wealth is used to exercise power over others, considerable hostility is generated.

It is equally difficult to participate in what might be described as the bottom end of the class spectrum. Much the same as in the U.S., one has to be a bona fide member of the working class. Since Australians have a high degree of respect for manual labor, more so even than Americans, they believe "a fair go" demands you judge a person on the basis of his or her inherent character traits rather than on education, wealth, or profession. In reality, class differences are relatively small in Australia, and any attempt to establish class barriers is strongly resisted. This is not the case in the United States and is often the source of conflict between the two cultures. Americans are, for example, more likely to distinguish groups or classes of people based on profession or education. Often, one of the first questions asked upon meeting someone is "What do you do?" Identifying where a person went to school is another way Americans determine the status of a new acquaintance. In Australia people flaunt their education at their own peril.

Language

In Australia, much more so than in the United States, language is a mixture of imaginative metaphor and swearing. It is, as the Australian writer John O'Grady states, "pungent, succinct, apt, sometimes explosive, frequently profane and always irreverent."

However, odd as it may seem, the Australian language does not provide the insight into class that language does in the United States or in Britain. Australian English is fairly uniform, without regional differences or dialects and with few variations in tempo. It's basically the same from Cooktown to Perth. Australians nevertheless acknowledge that the language as they speak it is not easily understood by others. Also, Australians have a habit of mumbling. The reason, some scholars in this land of many insects have suggested, is that Australians tend not to open their mouths when they speak so as to keep out the ubiquitous fly.

There is one connection between language and class in Australia. To be accepted by workers, one must have a command of "Strine." Strine, derived from "Australian," is an English dialect that is almost a distinct language in itself and adds to the communication problems Americans have with Australians because of the more general differences outlined above. The principal feature of Strine is the amassing and condensing of groups of words. For example, the question most often asked on Monday mornings:

"Djvagudweend?" (Did you have a good weekend?)

"Bludioth!" (Bloody Oath! [Yes])

Needless to say, an encounter with Strine can be quite disconcerting for other speakers of English. For their part, Australians have little difficulty understanding Americans and even occasionally experience a bit of frustration at the inability of Americans to understand "plain English."

Status

It is in the *overt acknowledgment* of superior/inferior status that the two countries mainly differ. Americans derive status from their company position and professional title and want the title used accurately. Australians react quite negatively to this kind of demonstration of status. Thus, Australians—perhaps paradoxically since the differences between their classes are small and the tone of their society is generally democratic—have a higher degree of class-consciousness than do Americans. They are much more sensitive to class distinctions and inclined to deny them, to "cut down the tall poppy." This sensitivity causes Australians to be very much aware and often intolerant of the more obvious class distinctions they encounter in the United States. They particularly resist being categorized themselves, especially when they perceive the status assigned to them as lower than their counterparts and the treatment they receive as condescending. This may reflect feelings of inferiority in relation to Americans, which some people believe are part of the Australian psyche and which seem to be manifested sometimes in a "little brother" syndrome toward "big brother" America.

Because of their egalitarian ideology, one is able to approach most Australians, no matter how high their position, with the certainty of an attentive, cordial hearing. Nowhere in the world do employers and employees mix socially more readily than in the numerous clubs where the two groups regularly meet and drink together. One is more likely to approach an American of high position with some reticence, some sense of imposition, some awareness of the demands upon the person's time (which may also reflect a difference in the way time itself is valued), if indeed one can gain access to the person in the first place.

Income distribution is far more equal in Australia; the difference between the top and bottom 5 percent is twice as great in the United States. Basic "benefits" (financial support) are provided as a "right" to students and to all those who are unemployed, hospitalized, or retired.

Australians tend to be less conspicuous in their acquisition and consumption of material goods than are Americans, a trait which is as much culturally as economically or technologically determined. A joke told by an American expatriate goes like this:

"What's the difference between Australia and the U.S.?"

"Oh, about ten years."

There are some technologies not as widely available in Australia as in the U.S., but there is also less of an inclination to accumulate them as eagerly. The Australians counter the American joke with one of their own. The wife of a soon-to-be-relocated senior American executive expressed to her Sydney realtor her disappointment at not being able to find a kitchen with a garbage compactor. The realtor's response: "In Australia we call a garbage compactor a 'foot'!"

Violence is less apparent in Australia, but it is on the increase, mainly in areas where youth unemployment or racial tension is extreme. Mugging of the innocent remains rare. In American culture physical violence is more widespread and causes considerable concern for overseas visitors, including Australians. Few actually encounter it in person, however.

From early on America has seen itself as a cultural melting pot. While it is now experiencing severe social stresses because of the large number of "unmeltable ethnics"—blacks, Hispanics, Asians, and Native Americans—there is a basic commitment to pluralism in the American value system. The racial/cultural makeup of Australia is also beginning to change, but this change is recent, beginning only after World War II, when new immigration was welcomed. At first the net was cast only among countries in Europe—"folks like ourselves"; then it was extended to southern Europe and then to the Middle East. With the ending of the White Australia Policy in 1973, the net covered the whole world, including Asians, from whom Australians have always feared inundation if they ever liberalized their Asian immigration policies. Asians made up two-thirds of Australia's 1988 immigration quota. Nevertheless, Australians have little experience with cultural pluralism. The government's official policy of multiculturalism has been a political necessity to meet the demands of non-Europeans already living there, but it has no teeth. Australia certainly still *looks* Anglo, even though Melbourne has more Greeks than any city outside Athens, part of Sydney (Marrickville) is 80 percent Turkish, and Cabramatta is predominantly Vietnamese. True multiculturalism lies ahead for Australia, and it is hoped that the new immigration policy will provide a drive and energy which will enable the society to adapt.

Social Relations

"Familiar, informal, attractive, open, but different—a kind of not-American American, a not-English Englishman," said an editorial about the Australians in the *National Geographic*. In this section we will examine in detail that more or less accurate impression of Aussies and contrast it with a view of Americans as they come across to others in social interactions.

Cooperation, Competition, and Leadership

The value systems of Australians and Americans combine competitive and cooperative strands, but in different ways. The Australian harmonizes them while the American sees them as mutually exclusive and is torn between them. Americans are always ready to put themselves in competition with the group or groups to which they belong; it is often "either the group or me." For the Australian it is "the group *and* me, with a great deal of personal privacy as well." Australians search for ways to collaborate with the competition while Americans seek ways to "beat" it. The American position seems to be that too much cooperation weakens one's advantage. This may stem, in part, from the different ways such values are inculcated. For example, much is made of mandatory participation in team sports in Australian schools. Americans place more emphasis on the outstanding individual and early on learn "spectatorism," with its powerful identification with the few superior performers. Social welfare legislation is much more comprehensive and more readily accepted in Australia than in the United States. The degree to which social welfare is a continuing social, political, economic, and ideological battleground in the United States surprises Australians.

From the beginning Australians were underdogs who had to cooperate to survive in a difficult situation. They developed a high degree of individuality, but whatever competitive spirit went with it tended to become merged with their underlying inclination toward cooperation. Americans have placed much more emphasis on personal independence, "rugged individualism," as it is called in the American belief system. They revel in fierce competition and usually agree to cooperate only on certain terms and for specific benefits or payoffs or for the achievement of a defined goal. These attitudes toward cooperation and competition are reflected in the different approaches to leadership in the two cultures.

"Australian conditions encourage fellowship rather than leadership," wrote H. M. Green, an Australian literary historian.[2] The homogeneity, cohesiveness, and involvement *with* one's fellows which Australians prize make them disinclined to value or express respect for exceptional qualities in individuals.

Americans, in contrast, emphasize the identification and reward of exceptional qualities—the ability to lead, to create ideas, and to manage an organization, or to perform well on tests, the athletic field, or the concert stage. Americans are encouraged to develop such qualities and to look for and respect them in others. It is to these people with exceptional qualities that Americans look for leadership, even though sometimes the exceptional nature of the qualities is hard to determine and the leadership provided is less than inspiring.

The implications of these differences in attitude are many, particularly in regard to personal relations between Australians and Americans. Americans are accustomed to being respected for what they consider to be their outstanding qualities—as a nation and as individuals—and believe that they deserve the mantle of leadership they wear. They are therefore confused, put off, and sometimes insulted when these qualities are not respected (and often not even acknowledged) by Australians. For their part, Australians feel put upon if they sense that their American associates expect them to accept American leadership and to admire American qualities they care little about. In Australia one leads by fostering cohesiveness and the fellowship of mutual involvement.

Levelers vs. Achievers

Their contrary approaches to leadership are also seen in their differing attitudes toward status and achievement. Americans are quite conscious of their own status. They define status primarily in terms of occupation, income, and professional position. They work at achieving status, cultivating appropriate patterns of behavior, and acquiring the material goods and other symbols associated with it. Americans are therefore usually willing to give at least qualified respect to someone having status.

Australians are also status-conscious, but in a different manner. Their sensitivity to the overt recognition of class and status, as discussed earlier, makes any indication of wanting to set oneself up as superior to one's fellows extremely distasteful. For example, even Liberal (the conservative party in Australia) politicians have been known to decline knighthoods from the Queen on the grounds that such titles are considered an electoral liability. Others have chosen to accept the title and have paid the price. Australians are suspicious of pretension, more so than Americans, and are critical of affectation. One report highlighting this difference concerned the first meeting of two academics. The Australian was affronted when practically the first question from the American concerned their respective degrees. "She's probably got more degrees than a thermometer," he recalled thinking. This affront was further exacerbated when the American woman went on to explain that her degree, in French, came from the *sixth* best school in the United States! The Australian reported that he wondered why she had bothered to provide that irrelevant and, he suspected, quite subjective piece of information. Who cared? His concern was whether or not this person could teach French. The Australian found out six months later that the American thought she was reassuring him about the quality of her credentials.

Newcomers from England in Australia have always received harsh treatment on this score and are called somewhat derogatorily "poms" or "pommies," the derivation of which is lost in history. Even the merest hint that they are comparing Australia with the "Old Country" brings them under attack.

Americans have also traditionally opposed old, especially European, forms of rank and status, but attitudes have mellowed with time and no longer have the virulence of an Australian's feelings on the subject.

Given their attitudes toward status and toward people who assume superiority, Australians are alert to pretensions in the Americans they meet and react negatively when they encounter them. What irritates Australians most is when Americans, by the way they behave, seem to be saying "We are the best and know the most." This manner derives partly from the fact that Americans place a high value on individual achievement, on rising to the top, on success; they feel that recognition, or status, is one's due. In American culture one is advised not to hide his or her talents.

In contrast, there is a strong leveling tendency within Australian culture that rejects any show of superiority or special talent. Even the "upper crust" avoids such displays. In the latter part of 1989, in fact, the Australian prime minister was roundly criticized in the Australian press for spending too much time with people like millionaire Alan Bond. When Australians bring their leveling tendencies into their relationship with Americans, conflict often occurs. Americans raise the hackles of their Australian acquaintances even though, in the context of their own society, they are not really "putting on the dog," as they are sometimes accused of doing by the Australians.

Controversy and Status

In conversations, Americans usually seek points of agreement and prefer to avoid subjects over which arguments might arise. By contrast, Australians revel in controversy and love to discuss subjects about which they disagree. As has been noted in the press, Australians are "famously straightforward" and don't mind passing and even taking an insult or two. The suddenness and vigor with which an Australian can come out with a strong or uncompromising position can be very disconcerting to Americans, who value even-temperedness and self-control and consider these fluctuations in behavior an indication that Australians are unpredictable and possibly unreliable. These reactions are particularly true of Americans in business, government, and higher education.

The American style of expression is related to a need to be liked, and Americans gain approval by agreement and support. Australians, partly because of their sometimes inconsistent behavior and sardonic manner and partly because they express respect by challenging, do not give the signals and reinforcements that tell Americans they *are* liked. Consequently, Americans often don't know where they stand with Australians.

Australians are less concerned than Americans about what others think of them; they are not as interested in whether anyone who isn't a "mate" (see discussion of "mateship" on page 31) likes them or not. Therefore, they do not try as hard as Americans to influence other people's opinions of them.

Americans assume that similarity fosters a friendly relationship. Eager to form relationships with Australians, they tend to concentrate on their common interests and practices. Australians, although they emulate some aspects of American style, see themselves (and want to be seen by others) as distinct from Americans. Therefore, while Australians are expressing in various (perhaps rather blunt) ways that they are different, the Americans are hearing "I don't like you." An American's motivation to cooperate may be linked to his or her need to be liked. Productivity could suffer and bad feelings could be generated from misinterpretation of an Australian's comments.

Americans tend to like people who agree with them. Australians are more likely to be interested in a person who *disagrees* with them; disagreement produces a lively conversation. Americans assume that disagreement implies rejection. Australians believe that disagreeing with someone has little to do with liking or disliking. Disagreement, in fact, can indicate sincere interest and respect. "The 'bloke' cares enough to really disagree with me." This makes Australians habitually brash stimulators of controversy, proud to own the local label of being a "stirrer." "Hey," they might say, "who do you think you're kidding? You Yanks are as clumsy in your argument as a duck in a ploughed paddock (field)." So when an American looks for agreement from an Australian and the Australian responds with disagreement, the American doesn't really like the Australian very much and, further, feels rejected. Such characteristic differences in style can turn a simple social gathering into a frustrating and demanding occasion. But it gets worse.

Conscious of status and wanting to be liked, Americans do things which they think will impress others. These are done naturally and with the expectation, based on experience with other Americans, of a favorable response. But they don't get it from their Aussie acquaintances. *It is very difficult to impress Australians.* Recall that Australians abhor anything smacking of pretension or status-consciousness. They quickly become impatient with attempts to impress them. When asked what they find most difficult to understand about Americans, Australians will often reply, "their obsession with making a good impression." An American, expecting a favorable response but receiving something quite different, is left confused and disconcerted.

Australians often display a somewhat sardonic demeanor and can be cynical to the point of assuming in almost any situation that something or other will almost certainly go wrong. But that's okay; life can be good even in the midst of failure. Americans, on the other hand, will work on details and worry over them endlessly, striving to make sure things don't go wrong. Australians don't think it's worth the effort. "We'll work it out somehow when the situation arises," they are inclined to say. When they display their contempt for the kind of fuss and excessive worry and diligence Americans put into what the Australians consider the finer points of protocol and procedure, disharmony or worse is the likely result.

Underlying many of these points of difference and difficulty is a difference in focus. When trying to get a sense of who a person is, an Aussie looks for inherent qualities. An American is more likely to look at what the person does and has done. When sizing up someone in a professional setting, an Australian concentrates on the person's competence and the qualities which lie behind that competence. An American more often concentrates on the person's accomplishments and on the position or positions the person has held, including the number of people and the amount of money over which the person has jurisdiction. Aussies will say, "A Yank talks like a resumé, instead of letting you know who he really is." Because of this difference in focus, misconnections between Australians and Americans are common, though often unrecognized.

More interested in personal qualities, Australians frequently find simply boring those Americans who want to let their achievements and position speak for them and who try to be friendly and agreeable—nice, but not very engaging or challenging. In order to evoke more tangible reactions from the American and thereby enjoy an exchange of substance and color, the Australian will become very candid or direct, at which point the American is more likely to withdraw than respond. When the Australian becomes even more emphatic, with a comment like "Well don't just stand there looking like a stunned mullet (fish), say something!" the American excuses him- or herself to get another cocktail. "Why," Australians sometimes ask, "are Americans so afraid to show their colors?"

Australians have other reasons for being assertive. They gain needed recognition and develop and confirm their sense of themselves by thinking and acting *against* others and against others' opinions, pretensions, and expectations. As Rupert Murdoch put it, Australians want to take on the world, in part because they have a great need to prove themselves. Americans, on the other hand, increase their self-esteem by acting *in accord with* the actions and expectations of others. Australians and Americans, in other words, are reinforced and supported by quite opposite responses from other people. Therefore, when an Australian (who wants someone to push against) is with an American (who wants someone to move along with), the Australian thinks the American is wishy-washy, and the American thinks the Australian is overbearing and obnoxious.

Given these contrasts in how Australians and Americans try to know others and affirm themselves, it is understandable that (frequently) after the first impressions wear thin, neither finds relations with the other very satisfying.

Trust and Respect

It follows, from the different bases on which they accord status and respect, that Australians and Americans trust (and distrust) persons for different reasons. Australians tend to base their trust on the capacity for loyalty and commitment a person has and on *their own* sense and estimation of that person. Americans tend to base their trust on the person's capacity for performance and consistent behavior, and on *other people's* recognition, ranking, and accreditation of that person. When interacting with Americans, therefore, Australians base their trust of the Americans on their own assessment of the individual's personal (internal) character. Americans, however, tend to base their trust on the Australian's professional or role (external) characteristics. An American, for example, is more inclined than an Australian to trust a person simply because he or she is a surgeon, baby-sitter, mechanic, or executive. Of course, anyone who violates a trust because of personal character weakness will not be trusted again. For Americans, then, putting trust in someone is more a test of character than a judgment of it. Like many aspects of interpersonal behavior, this mode of establishing trust is very likely related to social and geographic mobility. Americans need to assess trustworthiness quickly. They encounter too many unfamiliar people and have too little time to do otherwise.

Closely related to trust is respect. Here again there are important differences. Given their inner direction and their sense of natural equality, Australians respect character wherever it is found. Americans more often respect past and potential accomplishments, whatever the nature of the accomplishments. Australians recognize and respect individual worth apart from status. For them what matters is the kind of person you are rather than what you have done. In particular they like a person whom they term a "battler." As Australian author Bill Horndage put it, "A man is judged by the way he measures up to life (not work). And the bloke who does his best at all times, the bloke who is an unlucky poor bastard but who can smile, who can still find reserves of strength and courage to try again, is a battler."

The different bases of trust and respect account, in part, for the difficulty Australians and Americans have in knowing whether the other is sincere. Australians sometimes say that the most difficult thing to figure out about Yanks is whether they are "fair dinkum" (genuine) or not. They wonder: "Are Americans sincere about what they say?" For their part, Americans puzzle: "What must I *do* to impress Australians?" The answer: as little as possible; just act natural and be patient. Australians will not be pushed or hurried.

Consistency and Contradiction

Human beings are given to inconsistency. Americans wish it were not so and try to avoid contradictions. They like predictability and are accustomed to role-conforming behavior.

Nonconformity is admired in the abstract because it is identified with individualism, but in real life, the nonconformist may simply be annoying. Contradictions that appear *within* an individual make Americans especially uncomfortable because they interfere with the process of categorization that renders people comprehensible and predictable.

Americans are reluctant to accept contradictions either within themselves and their own behavior or within others. Australians, in contrast, are not normally bothered by contradictions. Indeed they are themselves often contradictory and like it if you tease them about it.

One of the most pronounced and disturbing contradictions Americans encounter in their Australian counterparts lies in their mood shifts. Predicting at any given moment whether an

Australian will be taciturn or outspoken, reserved or volatile, is almost impossible for Americans and keeps the relationship between the two continuously off balance. But there is a key. Australians will tend to be quiet or taciturn when the emotions they are experiencing—of pleasure *or* of pain—are deep. About things that are not very significant they will be much more spontaneous and uninhibited. Thus, when Australians are talking, even in their usual low-key style, no matter how offensive, harsh, or abusive, don't worry. When they are more quiet than normal, take care; there may be a serious problem.

Australians are contradictory in other ways. They are, for instance, at once rash and prudent. They have a penchant for cool, extravagant gambling (in lotteries, horse racing, and the national game of "two-up" or flipping coins), but, at the same time, they save more money per capita than most other people in the world; savings banks proliferate, and life insurance investment is high. A majority of Australians are determined to own their own homes as they strive for middle-class stability and security.

Such contradictions are disturbing for Americans, who tend to deal with the world in "either-or" terms—you're either for me or against me; you either like me or don't like me—and determine their response accordingly. Confronted with the contradictions they encounter in Australians, Americans often feel ambivalent and maintain their distance. "What is really behind the Aussie's actions?" they ask themselves.

Ideals and Principles

Americans and Australians are both pragmatic, and both base their behavior on principles or ideals. Yet, there is a vast gulf between them in the ways in which they manifest the principles in their lives. Derived to some extent from their relatively strong religious traditions ("American life makes no sense without religion," said President Lyndon Johnson in 1965), Americans see their lives governed by ideals: justice, freedom, equality, the sanctity of the individual and of private property. Americans learn these principles from an early age; they are enshrined in the nation's historical documents; and they constitute the framework within which national political and social debates are carried on.

In Australia, ideals seem to fall within the domain only of preachers, labor union leaders, and mothers. For the men, fairness is the simple, all-pervasive norm. "Come on, give us a fair shake!" is usually enough to gain compliance—or is at least the most potent argument—in situations where disagreement is strong, though little attention is given to the relative apportionments needed to ensure fairness. The result is a mix of tolerance and agreement which produces a workable compromise without any extended debate.

Americans are more complex. They depend upon quite explicit norms, frequently couched in absolute terms, but at the same time they are very pragmatic and are ready to resolve differences and disagreements over principle in a practical process of negotiation and compromise. But the ideals do not lose their force. To many Australians, who are less inclined to articulate their principles, arguments over ideals would be considered hot air. "A bloody waste of time. Let's forget it and have a beer, and leave that stuff to the few 'wowsers' (puritanical fanatics) left in this country who still go to church!"

Successful interaction between Americans and Australians demands that each tolerate the other's attitudes toward ideals and principles; in practice, of course, behavior is guided by a sense of common decency, and in this matter, thankfully, the two are not far apart.

Style of Conversation

Australians have developed and appreciate the art of deadpan understatement. Americans, who tend to take spoken words literally (except when they themselves use exaggeration and overstatement—which they do often), rarely comprehend the full meaning and intent of an Australian's understatements. For example, after winning the men's singles championship at Wimbledon, an Australian tennis player responded to praise with: "I guess I had a few lucky breaks." Neither criticism nor praise is lavishly bestowed by Australians. If it is, you're either very close to the other person or very much of an outsider (and the praise is probably sarcasm).

Americans, who tend to be expansive in their conversation, also have difficulty understanding Australians because they are often laconic. Concerning a new product, an American might say, "With the state-of-the-art technology we use, our widget is probably the best in the world," and then go on to give details, while the Aussie would likely as not say simply, "Oh, our widget isn't too bad, considering," and then wait for questions before providing details.

Not only do styles of conversation differ, but attitudes toward conversation differ as well. Americans tend to place consider-able importance upon the exact words exchanged and upon the topic. Australians do not; indeed, just the contrary. As Brian Fitzpatrick, a distinguished Australian historian, stated (especially in regard to Australian men):

> Utterance is better not done at all; but if it is done, when it is done, it were well it were slowly, flatly and expressionlessly to betoken that the subject, any subject, is hardly worth talking about.

While Americans are as inclined as people in any culture to make negative comments about other people, they seldom make them about people they are with, and they are uncomfortable when others do. Australians often express negative feelings about people they are with. For example, when someone does something a little untoward, they would think nothing of saying "You're as balmy as a 'bandicoot' (a big rat)." This is probably why Americans sometimes complain about Australians being brazen and sarcastic. It is important for the American visitor or businessperson to appreciate the Australian tradition of outra-geously free speech. It is a right that, unlike in the United States, is given no protection by the Australian constitution. It is simply taken for granted by the society. An Aussie hardly hesitates when only slightly put off to say jocularly, "What a silly bugger you are." For example, in an October 1989 nationally televised speech to constituents, the Australian prime minister responded to an elderly man who complained angrily about his pension with: "I don't know what you're talking about, you silly old bugger!" Australians, by and large, would not and, indeed, did not find this offensive. If an American politician made this kind of remark, there would be a media storm and significant political consequences.

Americans have, and often use, a variety of terms which create an air of objectivity or have a nonspecific, noncommittal, positive tone. Australians, on the other hand, use hundreds of casual, colorful terms in a teasing tone of amiable, tolerant contempt. When Americans take these remarks out of their Australian context and interpret them as if an American had said them, they are likely to think Australians are crude, critical, and conceited. At a minimum they are likely to be uneasy lest the Australians evaluate them negatively, failing to recognize the fact that willingness to express negative feelings may, for the Australian, be a way of showing respect—which must never be stated explicitly.

Humor

Both Australians and Americans enjoy and appreciate informal, spontaneous humor. Australians, however, feel that humor is appropriate (and even essential) in a wider variety of situations than do Americans. Also, Australians inject their humor with a certain amount of cynicism, which Americans often find harsh or even offensive. Australian humor may come across to Americans as inappropriate to the situation or disrespectful. An Australian asked by his American boss, "Would you do me a little favor?" shot back, "It depends what the favor is"—a piece of Aussie humor which, he reported, backfired. In response to a serious (and rather lengthy) speech by an American engineer, two Australians responded, "Garn, I don't believe you!" and "You don't bloody say." The American's reply was a smiling "I guess I was a bit long-winded, but it's really vital to our success...."

Australians, in turn, feel that Americans tend to be too serious and that their humor is constrained and lacking in color and spice. Each therefore has some difficulty understanding and responding to the humor of the other.

Humor with sexual overtones can also cause problems. Americans of both sexes participate in a more or less innocuous flirtation game. Australians are likely to take such comments seriously and respond with sexual advances.

Fundamental differences between two peoples are often revealed when they are under stress. Americans under stress tend to roll up their sleeves and dig in, concentrating more intensely and becoming more serious. An Australian under stress is more likely to begin making jokes to lighten things up a bit. Americans also joke to ease tensions, but as the pressure increases, they bear down harder and expect others to as well. The Australian sees more that is ironic and funny and takes the situation less seriously, no matter how bad it is. At those very points, therefore, that the American expects sober attention to the task at hand, the Australian leans back and tosses off a clever quip. Each is solving the same problem in his or her own way. The one finds satisfaction in the end result; the other seeks it each step of the way and, through the use of humor (poking fun at oneself if need be), stays on top of whatever comes, even if it is less satisfactory than it could have been with greater application of sober-minded diligence and attention.

"Mates" and Friends

Precisely what does the Australian mean by the term *mate*, which is used so frequently? *Mateship* has disputed origins. Some trace it to the arrival of the first exiles, others to the time when the new Australians were gathered to work in the gold fields some seventy years after the initial settlements. At both points a show of egalitarianism and expressions of mutual dependence made one feel a little more secure under very stressful conditions.

Mate is a masculine synonym for "friend," "buddy," or "pal." He could be a close coworker, teammate, or neighbor. A father will call his son mate; a grandfather, his grandson. It is a compliment for one man to refer to another as "a mate of mine." Mateship emerged from mutual need but over time grew in mythical dimensions. But as social historian Ronald Conway suggests, "Mateship has always been primarily a utilitarian matter, a relationship not to be equated with sustained same-sex bonding. It consists of a common expectation of support which facilitates the connection, rather than any sharing of oneself." That expectation of support can exist in any relationship between Australians who suddenly share a challenge. Though it should not be equated with same-sex bonding, it is always a part of very close friendships. While the term is most commonly used concerning male-male relationships, it can be female-female, and possibly the deepest compliment a man can pay his wife is to call her his mate.

"Mate" rather than "sir" is still the most common form of address because it is also a generic label. It can be used for the petrol station attendant or for any male stranger that you meet. It becomes a polite form of address man to man: "Hey mate, how do I get to Coonabarrabran?" The meaning changes with context, but Australians are never confused by the shades of meaning. In its most specific sense, a "true" mate is a fellow mate on whom one can place absolute reliance. Doing favors is part of mateship but, more importantly, so are obligations. Feelings of obligation are less strong in American friendships, though Americans too tend to view friendships as utilitarian. Being so preoccupied as they often are with getting something done, Americans tend to value a relationship because it is useful to some external end. While mateship among Australians is, Conway continues, also utilitarian, it embodies an idea of mutual support that focuses on and strengthens the personal aspect of the relationship rather than something external to it. A mate is anyone who will lend a hand, ranging from lifelong intimates to the newly met. And woe betide those who accept the help but ignore the resulting obligation.

The American when in trouble will tend to look to a professional for support or solace rather than inconvenience his or her friends. There appears to be a sense that real friends will listen to immediate problems but should not be burdened by long-term concerns which are better dealt with by professionals or a support group. Americans place such great value on independence that they hesitate to risk the kind of dependency relationship that might result from seeking help from friends when major problems arise. This feeling that the individual must be responsible for him- or herself also explains—at least in part—the widespread concern among Americans with self-improvement and with developing the skills needed to solve one's own problems. One government study some years ago found that approximately 10 percent of Americans were getting professional counseling or therapeutic help, while another study, reported in *Newsweek* in January 1990, indicated that 15 million Americans attended self-help groups weekly, and this did not include those who were in professional counseling or therapy groups.

One of the most important factors making for different friendship patterns between Australians and Americans lies in the social evolution of the two cultures. Specifically, small-town values and relational styles have been less eroded in Australia than in the United States. This is partly because most Americans, but only a minority of Australians, live in a city other than that of their birth. Although the trend is toward a more impersonal existence, Australians predictably will continue to spend their lifetime in the same metropolitan area. This both allows and requires one to adopt patterns of interaction which will be maintained over a long period of time as comfortable and satisfying relationships. By contrast, Americans are very mobile. One-fifth of the American people move every year. They are by necessity continuously selecting, developing, and terminating relationships. In the stable towns that characterize Australia, one can let relationships develop slowly and be assured they will have the chance of lasting a lifetime. Thus, in Australia one's personal reputation for being "counted on" or for carrying out one's obligations becomes a part of the relationship. Americans, on the other hand, must be able to develop relationships quickly and wisely and be able to break them without excessive personal disruption. Friendships among Americans tend to form around common interests rather than proximity or long-term acquaintanceship. For Americans, what they are *doing* is very important, so much so that their sense of self incorporates what they do, especially what they achieve. Consequently, American and Australian professionals have different criteria for constructing friendships. The American, stressing what a person does, finds the Australian too passive; the Australian, concerned with who a person is, finds the American too superficial.

A second major factor influencing how each of the cultures works out its style of interpersonal relations is the way they communicate and engage in self-expression. Americans, as we have noted, say much; Australians say little. Americans overstate; Australians understate. Americans express feelings; Australians imply them and are more private about them. These stylistic differences not only affect *how* friendship is expressed, but also *what* aspects of it are considered important.

What results from these and other influences are attitudes and behavior that characterize and differentiate Australian and American friendship patterns. Americans tend to be skilled at *initiating* new relationships—for at least two reasons: (1) they feel they need to cast the net as widely as possible to maximize the chance of finding good candidates for closer relationships and (2) they must do so quickly and efficiently in each new situation where the stay might be too short to allow such things "to take their own time," as a birth-to-death Brisbaneite might.

In this friendly initiating behavior Americans appear to foreigners to be making overtures to friendship or, for Aussies, mateship. For Americans, however, this behavior results in more or less superficial acquaintanceships which may or may not develop into friendships. Having misread the cues, Australians often accuse Americans of being superficial in their human relationships. In fact, for many reasons, Americans tend not to have significant numbers of close friends, but the friendships they do have are not necessarily superficial.

American friendship patterns are more deliberate than those of Australians, who are much more spontaneous. Spontaneity

comes later for Americans when greater trust has been built up—
at which point they are ready to share confidences. But it is just at
this level of trust and sharing of confidences that Australians
become wary. They are reluctant to "share their guts" with anyone who is not a lifelong friend. Americans, on the other hand,
share confidences or engage in self-exposure more readily than
Australians as a means of deepening (and almost testing) the
relationship. Australians in marriage as well as same-sex bonding
often have to guess at the other's deepest feelings.

At the risk of oversimplifying, it would not be unfair to say
that the typical forty-year-old Australian will have many mates,
a few best mates, and a number of relatives with whom he or she
is very close. The typical forty-year-old American will have
many acquaintances and friends (all of whom are called
"friends"), one or two close friends or intimate relationships
(one of which is the spouse), and family ties largely maintained
courtesy of AT&T, the American telephone giant.

Cross-cultural relationships between Australians and Americans can be strongly affected by this contrast in relational styles.
They may start off well with the American open and friendly
and the Australian responding in open and spontaneous ways.
But from there it can be all downhill, as the Australian reacts
negatively to the deliberate behavior and the restraint that lies
just beyond the friendly, outgoing face the American presents
and as the American feels pressured by the sense of obligation
demanded by the Australian. If they get beyond that, they then
have to deal with the Australian's inclination to let the friendship develop slowly and without a great deal of self-expression
while the American, moving at a faster pace, becomes more and
more personal and expects the same from the Australian.

Women and Men

Beliefs concerning the proper relationship between men and
women vary radically among Australians, particularly those
identified as middle-class.

On the one hand, the idea is still widely accepted that women exist to serve men. On the other, feminists such as Australian writer Germaine Greer and pop singer Helen Reddy (whose proclamation "I Am Woman" is echoed worldwide) represent an awakening in at least a small vocal group—which is resented by many, both men *and* women. Australian women, for the most part, seek and find fulfillment in the home (but would rarely say, "I am *only* a housewife"). Socializing is still largely segregated; and around the ubiquitous "barbie" (barbecue), men and women still gather in separate groups.

When the first settlements were established, women were a small minority and were abused. Sixty years later they were still outnumbered three to one. Nevertheless, over the decades women have entered the work force relatively freely, and forty years ago the percentage of women employed in professional and technical positions in Australia was larger than in the U.S. In the work world today women usually receive fair treatment and are respected and rewarded according to their ability. Yet their admission to the professions now lags behind their U.S. counterparts as does their proportion in the work force. Male blue-collar workers in Australia still make much of an assumed superiority. Even within management one finds a smattering of individuals described by a male Aussie journalist as "chauvinistic idiots."

Australia's chauvinist orientation can pose problems for business or professional women from the United States who are assigned to Australia to work in traditionally male fields. This is further complicated if the woman's position is in management.

In a recent example, an American woman in personnel management was given a four-year assignment to the Australian office of a large U.S. multinational company. Ninety-five percent of the office employees were Australian, of which 75 percent were male. "The first two years," she reported, "were nearly impossible." If the Australian office had not had an American (male) general manager, she said, she would simply have gone home. The last two years, while still difficult, were easier because ground rules for gender relationships were gradually established.

Despite the better atmosphere in the United States, American women encounter comparable problems. An Australian banker on assignment in the northeastern part of the United States was told that it would be inappropriate for her to represent the bank at a business meeting with a particularly aggressive group of males from a southern bank—whom she would also have to entertain. It was felt that a woman, especially a blunt and direct Australian woman, would not be as effective in closing the deal as an American male. The woman handled the meeting well and reported that while the men were both uncouth and sexist, they were no worse than a number of Australian clients she had had to deal with. She was upset, however, by the attitude of her superiors that her sex and cultural background made her less suitable for the job.

Relations at Work

Commitment to Work

Among the many differences between Yanks and Aussies, those revolving around attitudes toward work are especially striking. An Australian, it is said, considers work to be a bloody nuisance and therefore does as little of it as slowly as possible. While in general Australians respect manual labor, their respect for *hard* work is qualified, and they are particularly reluctant to expend effort on any activity considered unnecessary, such as, in the words of A. L. McLeod, "standing up straight if there is a handy post to lean on." They have some of the shortest working hours in the world and the longest vacations.

"An Australian becomes aware at an early age that work is a national joke," explains Robert Haupt, Washington correspondent for the Australian *Financial Review.* "People who work hard are as likely to attract suspicion as praise." "If you stand tall enough on Monday, you can see Friday on Tuesday" is a saying which typifies the Australian attitude toward work.

But there are limits on the degree to which Australian workers will be "laid back." They especially frown on "bludgers" or freeloaders who are seen as not carrying their weight and as taking advantage of their mates (as distinct from the company). It's okay to have a bit of a bludge, for example, to take a "smoko," a breather for a smoke when time may not allow, but to be known as a bludger is one of Australia's strongest terms of reproach. Using the word loosely can cause a fight.

But given their general orientation, it is clear that Australians do not share the same work ethic as Americans. Their motto is to do enough to get by; people who work hard and make a point of letting others know it will be regarded with suspicion.

Americans, on the other hand, especially business executives and professionals, approach their work from a different perspective. They are much more likely to get a deep sense of satisfaction and strong feelings of self-fulfillment from it, to the degree that other aspects of their lives may be neglected. For many American men, their achievements in the workplace reinforce their sense of masculinity. These attitudes are, of course, derived to a significant degree from the strong work ethic that characterized the beliefs of many of the early European settlers in America. It was encouraged by a free enterprise system that rewarded hard work and a social ethic in which one could rise from poverty to wealth solely on the basis of that work. This philosophy provided American industry with a disciplined work force and became one of the principal criteria by which managerial capability was judged.

The long hours at the office, the stuffed briefcase lugged home each evening, the pressure of deadlines and the overtime work put in to meet them, the manager who is at his or her desk for two hours each morning before anyone else arrives are characteristic patterns of American corporate working life. Such values are encouraged by the expectations of the company's senior management. In the words of David Ogilvy, chairman of the large American advertising firm, Ogilvy and Mather, "The best institutions keep their promises no matter what the cost in agony and overtime."[3] While such dedication and effort may be begrudged by some caught in the system, they are still respected and certainly considered when decisions on promotions are being made. To the Australian, this type of American is the epitome of a workaholic.

Americans often see Australians as lacking in commitment and self-discipline and, therefore, probably unreliable in a crunch. Americans believe deeply that they can do anything if they work hard enough at it. Australians feel that they can *probably* do anything, but that the effort and sacrificed leisure might not be worth the rewards. When there is a now-or-never situation, they work very hard, though they never make the kind of commitment to work that Americans do. This has important consequences for the expatriate manager. An Australian manager in America, for example, can appear to lack dedication while the U.S. manager in Australia might be portrayed as a "slave driver," a person without a heart.

In spite of these differences, there is evidence that while they are working in the United States with Americans, Australians recognize that the American style is the condition of success, and they adapt to it.

In sum, Americans tend to value the *amount* of work done, assuming its usefulness. Australians must be convinced of its *usefulness* first. Aussies argue that the general quality of their lives is more important than accomplishing tasks, especially since the extra output rarely justifies the effort.

It is useful to examine respective priorities of Americans and Australians in corporate management. Both consider the quality of their lives of central importance; but they define it differently. For the Americans, quality is found mostly in the private domain (home, spouse, children, education, recreation), plus the sense of being a worthwhile person, which "success" brings. For the Australian, quality of life has no particular focus: it is the way one lives every moment. One's private life is important to Australians, and they expect to get the same kind of satisfaction from *all* aspects of their lives, not just from their free time. More importantly, they expect the free time to be even better and so begrudge working overtime because it seems to bring nothing extra; it only takes away from the choicest part of life. Americans work the extra hours, and at a more intense pace, with less vacation time, because the sense of satisfaction in accomplishing a task is so strong and because they believe it will all pay off later. For the one it is the pure achievement coupled with the things the effort buys; for the other, it is the totality of life that is important.

Inner-Directed vs. Other-Directed

A fundamental distinction affecting their relations on the job (and elsewhere) is the tendency of Australians to be inner-directed while Americans are usually more other-directed. Australians often base their evaluations and behavior upon things inside themselves—their own feelings, preferences, and expectations. Americans are more likely to base their evaluations and behavior on things outside themselves—in corporate policy, the particular situation, or other people's expectations.

The conflict between those who are inner-directed and those who are other-directed can be especially noticeable in an organizational context. An American is usually more willing to conform to the structure, roles, and norms of an organization. An Australian is more likely to take organizational structure, roles, and norms more lightly and move quite easily outside or against them. In addition, Americans expect conformity from others, including Australians. Australians, however, are inclined to resist these expectations; if the Americans put pressure on the Aussies to conform, they resist more firmly. The Australian sees the American as critical and pretentious; the American sees the Australian as uncooperative and obstinate.

Because Australians are more inner-directed, they usually do not shift their approach, behavior, and expectations according to the class, status, or other external factors of those around them. Americans value social adaptability and are somewhat more willing (and better able) to make these kinds of shifts. Noticing the Australians' reluctance to make the same kind of adjustments, Americans often conclude that Australians are self-centered, disrespectful, and intolerant. The result: frustration and irritation for both.

Americans have not always been as other-directed as they are now. Self-reliance has been a key value from the time the first settlers began to spread across the continent. As the other-directed American has evolved in the twentieth century, a conflict in values has occurred. The issues involved in this conflict have been especially significant in corporate cultures where, as pressures increase to maintain their competitive edge (against, among others, one of the most other-directed cultures in the world—the Japanese), the demand for conformity increases too. In short, Americans have become less tolerant of those who don't fit in—especially those, like the Australians, who *won't* fit in (unless you provide them with acceptable reasons for doing so).

Measuring Up to Standards

Australians, given their more internal orientation, tend to be rather indifferent toward standards, which by definition are external guides to decision and action. Whether a person's performance or a product meets a particular standard is, therefore, of less concern to an Australian. "She'll do" or "She'll be right, mate," is heard in Australian offices, where people are less inclined, for example, to demand that a memo or letter with one error be retyped. The purpose of a memo, they feel, is to communicate a message and if the meaning is not compromised, then it is a waste of time and resources to do it again. Australians tend to be as relaxed about standards as they can get away with. For the American manager this can mean jobs done with only enough time, effort, and care to make them minimally acceptable, with the Australian handing over the work and adding—in the face of his or her superior's obvious disappointment—the hopeful injunction, "She'll be right, mate, she'll be apples." The Australian is a willing enough worker when he or she sees something has to be done but is usually a very poor planner who leaves all sorts of things to chance in a manner that can give ulcers to dedicated managers.

Americans, because of their more external orientation, their educational experience, and their organizational procedures (and, more recently, governmental regulation), are very conscious of and concerned about maintaining standards of efficiency, productivity, and profitability. This concern has been reinforced by the technological competition with Japan since World War II during which time the prevailing technical standards in a number of major American industries were found wanting.

Given their differing attitudes toward standards, Australians sometimes see Yanks as driven nitpickers, while Americans view Australians as negligent and sloppy.

During faculty meetings at an Australian university, for example, visiting American lecturers in the English department would regularly get into squabbles with their Australian colleagues because they felt Australians lacked standards for evaluating the students' written assignments and had no shared criteria for what constituted a proper format, outline, or paragraph structure. They also felt the Australians were unsystematic in their grading, careless, and disorganized. The Australians' response was to denigrate the American "sticklers." Clearly the two had different ideas of what constituted appropriate academic standards.

Laws and regulations are set up with the same basic intent as standards (namely, to induce conformity), and they therefore often evoke a negative response from Australians. This response is so strong that relaxing rules and regulations is substantially more effective in motivating Australians to work carefully than enforcing them is.

Americans legitimize organizational behavior by creating policies, forms, and procedures, which they treat as nonnegotiable. Australians create far fewer forms and procedures and even these are considered negotiable. (Something like a precise title indicating one's place in the organization, for instance, seems like nit-picking to them, especially since they don't place any value on titles as such.) One Australian working in a large U.S. multinational described his response to what he felt was his boss's obsession with proper forms. He would sometimes make two different copies of a memo he was circulating, one correct and the other "Australian." He would then distribute the correct version to everyone but his boss, who would receive the Australian version. When the expected response occurred, he would explain that he'd inadvertently given his boss the draft copy of the memo.

The differences between Australians and Americans in their attitudes toward standards in the workplace make it difficult for each to understand and do what the other expects; this is particularly true of Australian men working in the United States, who often experience a significant degree of role shock at the outset. The Australian expects a broad degree of latitude in his work, but when it is constantly corrected with (from the Australian's perspective) no inherent improvement in the outcome, a great deal of stress can result. In the end the Australian may lose his self-confidence and experience feelings of self-doubt when his own expectations, that is to say his desire to do a good job, are not met.

Authority

Australians tend to denigrate authority because it acts as an external guide to making decisions and taking action, and Australians are not comfortable with external controls. This attitude is perhaps best summarized by British journalist Paul Johnson, who wrote: "Hostility towards authority in all its forms is a living, if latent, Australian tradition, liable to spring into rampant action if the temperature and alcohol mix is right." Americans, on the other hand, are inclined to accept authority within limitations, abide by it where feasible, and ultimately acquire it for themselves. These contrasting attitudes are the source of much of the friction and irritation experienced by Australians and Americans when they are trying to work together.

The Australians' resentment of superiors, like their loyalty to equals, is deeply rooted and long-standing. It had its origins in the harsh rule and authoritarian rigidity of the early government administered from London, which was strongly resented. Defying authority became a national habit for Australians. As John O'Grady notes, "Most of them have no respect for constituted authority, very little for tradition and none at all for the language."[4] Anyone in the group who rose to a position of authority, even a minor one, or displayed some excellence was likely to be reviled by his mates as a "scab" or "traitor." The comfortable leveling into mateship satisfies the need for security among Australians and is manifest in their attitude toward authority. Even the outlaw bushrangers like Ned Kelly (roughly the equivalent of Billy the Kid) are seen as folk heroes (Kelly was called "Highwayman Extraordinaire" and "Robber Deluxe"). Thieves though they were, they stuck by each other and they also "stuck it to" authority figures. Nothing brought them and their admirers greater pleasure than success in confounding the constabulary. The term "Ned Kelly" is still used in a number of contexts and is often applied to super salesmen types or to anyone who overcharges for something. "Who said bloody Ned Kelly was dead?" the victim will say. But to tell someone that they are "game as Ned Kelly" suggests that he or she is prepared to take on the world (and its controllers) and is a comment of high praise.

No matter how competent or effective the Australian employee may be, or how reasonably the power may be exercised, limited input into corporate strategic or financial plans may cause a kind of rebellion among the Australians, resulting in a decline in morale and a decrease in output.

The authority Australians resent is really any "they" who seemingly threatens them, their security, or their self-esteem. Thus, Australians are not, under their friendly demeanor, a tolerant people. Diversity of outlook easily brings anxiety and sometimes resentment, as many immigrants (known belittlingly as "wogs") can attest. It is no accident that many in the state of Queensland are proud of its former premier's overt racism, even

though other Australians disparaged Queensland as the "Ba-
nana Republic."

Americans were a rebellious lot too when it came to the
British crown. But while Americans have a long history of
belittling authority (with their frontiersmen and Western out-
laws representing an impulse similar to that of Australian
bushrangers) and have written into their Constitution many
safeguards against its excesses, they have also given a great deal
of conscious attention to the structures of authority they have
developed. Respect for the law and the freedom it provides is
perhaps the fundamental authority structure in the United
States. The Supreme Court is living witness to the determina-
tion to live by laws that are just, with concomitant authority
figures and institutions. During this century, the structures of
authority in government, business, and other organizations have
become especially important in American society for the stability
and continuity they provide, while the authority of the family
and of ethnic and religious communities has declined. Americans therefore tend to respect structures of authority; they are
accustomed to them and need them as a predictable framework
within which to function.

Today, many overseas U.S. senior managers feel that regardless
of the dedication and commitment of Australian employees, they
are so far removed from the central planning process and the
company's "global vision" that they cannot fully appreciate why
certain corporate decisions are made. Instead, country managers,
and those who report to them, are expected to follow headquarters' guidance. This can result in strained relations between the
subsidiary and the U.S. home office because of the Australians'
natural resistance to being told what to do. The whole thing can
get even more complex and result in more problems if the corporate headquarters adopts a "functional" approach to global management. This means that corporate headquarters has assigned an
individual to each major business function instead of allowing
the respective country managers to have final authority. A number of U.S. firms are taking this approach and, in the Australian

context, it allows even less access to senior management and its thinking and places them in the position of once again being managed by a distant "them."

Related to the question of authority is that of *accountability*, a matter of pervasive concern in American business and industry. Americans accept and insist upon accountability; Australians regard it with some reservations and often resist it. In Australia, if elected officials fail to fulfill election promises, they are rarely held accountable for them as they are more likely to be in the United States. When products are faulty, the consumer in Australia often swears but then forgets, whereas the American may storm in and demand a replacement. Australians are not taught accountability; they learn early to be casual about the untoward consequences of their behavior—"Mum," "the Wife," or "Hubby" will fix it up. The American concern for accountability feeds their preference for taking to the law over grievances. With the largest number of lawyers per capita in the world, the United States has become the most litigious country in the world.

Control is also an essential factor in any discussion of authority. Americans are usually more conscious of, and concerned about, control than are Australians. The intensification of competition both at home and abroad, the increasing complexity of managerial tasks, and the awareness that more and more of what concerns them is now *beyond* their control (the environment, basic resources, the international economy, etc.) have impressed the importance of control upon Americans. Control over personnel, among other factors of production, is therefore being given more careful attention in the United States than in Australia, where the individual is more resistant to and resentful of being controlled.

As was true with questions of trust and respect, Australians will accept authority and control (albeit reluctantly) if they consider the person exercising authority to be competent and interesting—to have, in a word, character. This takes time to establish and develop. American managers often fail to put in the time necessary to win the respect of their subordinates. What the Australian most often sees is the "nose to the grindstone" as soon as the assignment begins. If the manager moves too quickly in the overt exercise of authority, conflict can result. An American's acceptance of control is based more upon the particular position exercising the control and the amount of authority associated with it (and probably some thought as to where compliance will get him or her) than on the character of the person holding the position.

It is the concern Americans have—at least compared to Australians—for status, hierarchy, deference, and positions of authority that sometimes gives Australians the feeling that they cannot develop direct and comfortable relationships with Americans. One Australian working in the United States, for example, explained that the most irritating thing about Americans for him was "their reluctance to lower their guard, to just be themselves."

Instead of obeying, Australians are more accustomed to bargaining. When handed (or more often sent) instructions from an American, their sense of equality and fellowship is violated and their response is resistance. If approached personally and as equals, their experience and opinions considered, they are more inclined to engage and negotiate. Cooperation thus becomes the mode of interaction rather than argumentation and resentment. At the same time, it behooves Australians to resist the feeling of being denigrated every time they receive an impersonal memo or instruction. For the most part, Americans don't intend these to carry hidden meaning; it is an essentially neutral management style.

Decision Making

As one might suspect from the profile presented so far, Australians are collaborative in their orientation toward decision making. They believe quite strongly that decision-making procedures should be based upon management's assumption that subordinates share equal interests, organizational goals, and capabilities. They believe they should be consulted on major organizational decisions in order to reach corporate consensus. All information should be shared. This is what Australians call "industrial democracy."

Americans are somewhat less collaborative. They are inclined to believe that subordinates have less to contribute to organizational decisions and less right to make demands on management or the organization. It is assumed that senior management has the bigger picture. This pattern of decision making is changing in the United States as it becomes increasingly clear that the commercial and technological successes of the Japanese have stemmed significantly from a consensus style of business operations. The quality circle and other methods of drawing workers and staff into the decision-making and policy-development processes are becoming more widespread in American corporations. Generally speaking, however, the decision-making style is still top-down and is based on a quantitative approach focused on quarterly profits. Some Australian firms, such as those led by entrepreneurs Rupert Murdoch or Alan Bond, function in a similar way, but the vast majority of Australian firms still prefer a more consensus style of management.

Motivation

Since Americans so highly value individual achievement and derive so much of their self-esteem from it, it is hardly surprising that achievement serves as a strong motivating force in their lives. Many Americans are professionally very ambitious. They expend considerable energy, sometimes exhausting themselves, in trying to realize their ambitions, which involve the achievement of status and position and the acquisition of wealth and honors, including the recognition and acknowledgment by others of their accomplishments. Australians, in contrast, are not so eager to excel and tend to minimize the importance of prestigious positions, wealth, and honors—both their own and others'.

While Australians usually appreciate the industriousness of Americans, they are put off by what they consider American workaholism. When asked, for example, what they find most difficult to understand about Americans, Australians frequently respond, "Their drive and push in business, their complete dedication to the 'rat race' and to making money."

Achievement and position are often symbolized for Americans by the level of their salaries which provides more motivation for them than it does for Australians. Shorter work days, longer weekends, and lengthier vacations are stronger motivators for the Aussie, who enjoys the present.

Americans are also motivated by the challenge of and involvement in particular tasks and projects, that is, in the work itself. While personal relations with their associates are important and a source of satisfaction, Americans, being task-oriented, tend to concentrate more exclusively than Australians on the job at hand. Australians, although also usually concerned about the task at hand, tend to be much more focused on their personal interests and more aware of the personalities of others working with them. Good interpersonal relations with their supervisors seems to be a particularly strong motivator for Australians, as does support and encouragement from his or her spouse. One American civil engineer who was working on a highway project for a U.S. company in Australia was constantly amazed at the fact that the men under him would not work overtime, or would take days off at a time that was inconvenient for the firm. Particularly irritating was their complete nonchalance about deadlines, when his priorities were coming in "under time" and "under budget." This was a classic face-off of cultural differences.

Americans are future-oriented. Planning, for example, is a major preoccupation of the American and a fundamental function of American business and other organizations. Yet that planning is rarely long-term. Americans are aware of the need to think in longer terms, but the long-range dream takes a back seat to this quarter's balance sheet. That long-range planning takes second place is demonstrated clearly by the auto industry's decade-long delay in responding to the Japanese dominance of the small car market or the current total dependency upon Japan for VCRs.

Australians think even more in the short term than Americans. They are interested in the present and don't get anxious about the future or the need to plan for it. They are less willing to postpone satisfaction and enjoyment until some later time. An American who has worked with Australians, for example, said that the thing he found most difficult to understand about Australians is that "they seem to live only for today."

Seeing or at least sensing these differences in Australians, Americans are likely to view Australians as uninvolved in their work and even careless. Australians are likely to see Americans as uninvolved in their relationships and captives of "success" and of their desires for the future.

Taking Risks

Australians are sometimes seen as more willing to take risks than Americans are, which can make for less bureaucratic restraint, more innovation, and stronger lateral thinking.

Traditionally, Americans have been risk takers too. Scholars trace the risk-taking inclination to the migration of millions of people who pulled up roots and literally risked everything in a new land. While risk taking is still a significant feature of American behavior and thrives among small entrepreneurs, the rise of large corporations has tempered the impulse; size has begotten conservatism. Individuals in general have become more concerned with job security and predictable advancement than they were in the past. Americans thus may be a little uneasy with Australians who without hesitation stand ready "to have a go at a thing." It underlines the new American conservatism which contradicts the perception Americans have of themselves as the world's leading risk takers.

Giving Credit

Because of their egalitarian spirit and leveling inclinations, Australians are reluctant to give *anyone* praise or credit. While they do appreciate exceptional qualities in people, they will seldom acknowledge or commend them directly or publicly, even in the case of someone who is extraordinarily competent and possesses an engaging personality. Australians are especially reluctant to give Americans credit because Americans expect it and, in the Australians' view, already think too highly of themselves. Yet in the sardonic put-down—"If you keep that up, you'll get the hang of it—in time, mate"—they do give credit where it is due.

Pace of Life

In both their social and work relations, Australians have difficulty, as do people from many other cultures, with the pace of life maintained by most Americans. Easygoing themselves, Australians often feel pushed and pressured while living in the United States. As Germaine Greer put it, "Australia is so laid back as to be horizontal." The hectic pace of American life is hard to take. Americans are always in a hurry—to get things started, to get things done, to get where they're going, to return from where they have been.

For the Australian on assignment in the United States, the desire to do a good job and meet expectations comes into sharp conflict with a lifestyle that seems excessively demanding and personally debilitating. When asked what aspect of Australian culture would be best for Americans to adopt, one Aussie expressed the feelings of many: "Slow down the rush and enjoy life." Some Americans agree. In a 1977 study of immigration trends in Australia, 21 percent of the American immigrants interviewed said that the reason for their coming to Australia was because the pace of life was slower.[5]

Conflict

Given the basic characteristics of Australians and Americans, it is hardly surprising that conflict between them occurs with some frequency. Indeed, we have identified a number of particularly volatile points at which conflict is most likely to arise. But that doesn't end it, since the conflict may well be aggravated or intensified by the marked difference in the way members of each culture deal with conflict itself.

In general, Americans do not like interpersonal conflict. As children they are taught to control their tempers. In social and business situations raised voices are generally a source of embarrassment. In conversations they tend to avoid subjects about which there might be disagreement and avoid arguing when disagreements do surface—or if they do argue it will be temperately. When conflict does arise, Americans are tough and confrontational. They are disinclined to engage in friendly but vigorous debate in which the winner is the one who presents his or her argument with the greatest intelligence and skill.

Australians do not find conflict uncomfortable; indeed they will invite a good argument and will respect the person who carries it off with skill and gets the results desired. The Australian educational system, like the European, prepares the individual better for rational argumentation than does the American. Australians are, in fact, similar to Europeans in this regard, that is, they find the American attitude toward conflict and argumentation rather strange. This approach does have some unfortunate ramifications in their society, where it contributes to the extreme antipathy that exists between workers and employers which might be moderated by greater restraint. In general, however, Australians are more resilient in the midst of debate and less concerned with negative reactions from those with whom they are in conflict.

Labor Relations

We have examined cultural difference as they apply to interpersonal and business management issues. One additional area where culture can affect a successful business relocation, joint venture, or subsidiary is in labor relations.

The U.S. Department of Commerce lists over five thousand American firms operating in Australia, while over one thousand Australian firms have offices in the United States. The massive flow of U.S. capital into Australia has given the Australian worker a growing sense of dependency and, as noted earlier in this analysis, has caused an exacerbation of the Australians' feelings of inferiority in their relationships with Americans. This sense of dependency is justified by hard facts. The United States enjoys a large balance of trade surplus with Australia in goods, services, and invisible exports.

Australians have repeatedly expressed concern over what they feel is exploitation by one of the world's economic superpowers (with a market twenty times larger) at the expense of Australia's own development. The media take note regularly of American—and Japanese—acquisition of land and their domination of certain strategic industries, such as sophisticated computers.

There is also a perception among Australian union leaders that American industry will share only what is necessary to build or refine products while developmental technology and innovative techniques are kept as the preserve of the home company. That may be true, for in the face of fierce competition from countries to whom the United States gave extensive recovery aid and/or development assistance after World War II, Americans have felt they had to abandon the generous policy they pursued for forty years of freely giving away their trade and technological secrets. This change in policy is not only disturbing in itself, it is associated in the minds of many Australians with the tendency of American companies to exercise firm control in Australia and elsewhere over their foreign operations—which Australian workers resent.

Australian labor unions function differently from American unions, and it behooves American and Australian managers operating in the other's country to understand these differences—especially since many depend not simply on variations in procedure or structure but on the cultural orientation of the workers.

Collective bargaining agreements negotiated between labor unions and management in the United States set the conditions of employment. For example, terms of dismissal are not regulated by the government, but are usually spelled out in wage agreements. Australian workers, more sensitive to issues of personal security, feel the need for government intervention and protection from the arbitrary whim of management.

In the U.S., unions are less militant and strikes fewer, usually taking place only after negotiations have broken down. In Australia, the more aggressive unions strike more frequently and like to time the strikes so that they will cause the greatest disruption or inconvenience to their management adversaries. The postal union, for instance, will strike during the holiday season and construction workers, when the project they're on is nearing but has not yet reached completion.

But why the difference? Why are American unions weaker? In the United States, workers don't seem to be as antimanagement, nor are they as ideologically or politically charged as Australian unions. The tradition of the aspiring laborer ascending the economic ladder from worker to middle-class manager is stronger and more acceptable in the United States. Also, as the Australian Department of Trade has noted, American unionism is held in check by the intense individualism in American culture and by the concept of labor as being private property, something owned by the individual and to be used without interference from bureaucratic organizations, that is, government agencies and trade unions.

In Australia union influence thrives under a regulated industrial relations system where the closed shop is almost an article of faith. The unions look for worker input into management decisions and oppose policies which emphasize short-term profits at the cost of longer working hours. Extreme resistance is likely to occur whenever an Australian union senses a threat to its overriding goals: a slower pace of life, higher pay, a shorter work week, and more vacation time.

To be successful, U.S. managers in Australia will have to be more attentive to union and worker needs as Australians perceive them. They may have to modify their approach to decision making and build into their policies measures which accommodate the quality-of-life issues Australian workers feel are so important, even if it means shifting their emphasis from short- to long-term profits.

Australian managers in the United States may have to be a little less casual and collaborative and a little more authoritative in their decision making. They may also need to be more systematic in and give greater attention to their approach to labor negotiations, since there is substantially less government regulation and fewer decisions will have to be made outside the negotiating room.

Summary of Basic Contrasts between Americans and Australians

THEME	AMERICANS	AUSTRALIANS
Social Structure	*Optimistic and future-oriented	*Present-oriented
	*Higher degree of class structure	*Relatively few class differences; sensitive to class distinctions
	*Categorize others by status	*"Cut the tall poppy"
	*High degree of cultural pluralism	*Low degree of cultural pluralism
Cooperation and Competition	*Seek agreement	*Enjoy disagreement
	*Need to be liked	*Don't care what others think
	*Less assertive	*More assertive
Trust and Respect	*Based on position and qualifications	*Based on assessment of one's character
Consistency and Contradiction	*Reluctant to accept contradictions	*Not bothered by contradictions

THEME	AMERICANS	AUSTRALIANS
Ideals and Principles	*Idealistic but pragmatic	*Less idealistic; expect a "fair shake"
Style of Conversation	*Place importance on exact words *Objective, positive	*Terse, noncommittal, understated *Language colorful, disrespectful, often profane
Humor	*Appreciate informal, spontaneous humor in the right place Disinclined to use humor under stress	*Use humor frequently, often injecting a certain amount of cynicism or irony *Inclined to use humor under stress
Friendship and Interpersonal Relations	*Value accomplishments of others *Friends and membership groups change easily *Relationships develop and end quickly without excessive personal disruption *Friendship seldom includes a strong sense of obligation	*Value inherent qualities in others *Friends and membership groups take a long time to establish *Relationships are long-lasting and meaningful *Friendship involves a very strong sense of obligation

THEME	AMERICANS	AUSTRALIANS
Women and Men	*Less chauvinistic than in the past	*Still very chauvinistic but changing slowly
	*Establishment of equity sought through legislative process (ERA)	*Women's admission to professions is limited
	*Sexes mix freely in social gatherings	*Sexes at parties, etc., still separate
Commitment to Work	*Workaholic achievers	*Laid back
	*Work comes before friends	*Work rarely comes between friends
	*Overtime and extra effort accepted as part of the job	*Overtime not accepted unless the reason is extremely important
	*Value the amount done, assuming its usefulness	*Need to be convinced of usefulness before the value of work is seen
Inner- vs. Other-Directed	*Other-directed	*Inner-directed
	*Evaluate behavior based on things outside of self	*Evaluate behavior based on one's own feelings and preferences
	*More flexible	*Less flexible

THEME	AMERICANS	AUSTRALIANS
Standards	*Conscious and concerned about standards *Litigation, forms, procedures, and documentation standard *"Got to get it right"	*Concerned (but not nearly to the same degree) *Less litigation, less documentation *"She'll be okay"
Authority	*Respectful within limitations *Respect superiors *Like to be in control *Generally accept management decisions	*Disrespectful *Resent superiors *Resist control *Prefer to bargain with management
Decision Making	*Top down; senior management has "big picture" *Assume subordinates have less to contribute to organizational decisions *Information need not be shared	*Collaboration between management and employees *Assume subordinates share equal interests and capabilities *Information should be shared

THEME	AMERICANS	AUSTRALIANS
Motivation	* Achievement is important and is related to ambition * Salaries and bonus very important	* Achievement is not so important; position and honors are minimized * More free time very important, salary less so
Taking Risks	* Cautious risk takers	* Ready to have a go at a thing
Giving Credit	* "Give credit where credit is due" * Expect praise	* Only begrudgingly give credit * Do not expect praise
Pace of Life	* Easy-going to fast * In a hurry to get places * "Doing"-oriented	* Laid back to easy-going * Slow down the rush, enjoy life * "Being"-oriented
Conflict	* Uncomfortable with conflict * Avoid argument * Concerned about what others think	* Comfortable with conflict * Invite argument * Not concerned about what others think

THEME	AMERICANS	AUSTRALIANS
Labor Relations	* Unionized but becoming less so	* Highly unionized
	* Informal arbitration	* Formal arbitration
	* Official strikes generally at end of contract	* Many strikes at advantageous times
	* Terms of dismissal unregulated	* Terms of dismissal regulated

[1] Thomas Keneally, "The Australians," *Life* (February 1988): 38.

[2] Henry McKenzie Green, *The History of Australian Literature* (Sydney, Australia: Angus & Robertson, 1961).

[3] David Ogilvy, *Ogilvy on Advertising* (New York: Vintage Trade Books, 1985).

[4] John O'Grady, *Survival in the Dog House* (Sydney, Australia: Ure M. Smith, 1973).

[5] "Australia as a Multicultural Society," Submission to *Australian Population and Immigration Council on the Green Paper, Immigration Policies and Australian Population* (Canberra, Australia: The Australian Ethnic Affairs Council, 1977).

4

Managing Together

The peoples of these two countries whose cultures have similar roots but who have developed in quite different ways can build effective relationships both in their professional and personal lives. Attention to the following principles will help.

For Americans and Australians

Knowledge of Each Other. Americans and Australians need to learn more about each other, and both have had difficulty doing so for different reasons. American newspapers and news magazines seldom carry articles on Australia, and what articles there are usually deal with trivialities, a practice Australians consider negligent. Conversely, information about America and Americans flows rather freely into Australia. Australians therefore assume they know a great deal about the United States. They do, but primarily about those aspects to which the media give attention or which they encounter in American movies. As far as accurate knowledge about fundamental characteristics of the two cultures is concerned, neither is especially knowledgeable. As a result, both begin interaction with one another with a definite disadvantage. It is therefore important that they learn more about each other and (Americans especially) evidence a greater interest

61

in each other. In general Australians feel that their interest in the United States is already stronger than the reverse.

Communication

Use the tried and true communication skills with which all managers, at least, should be familiar. Listen carefully, seek clarification, give feedback, and accept and evaluate honestly the feedback you receive. Watch for differences in the definition of words. Above all, empathize. Using the information presented here, try to determine where the other person's perception of the situation differs from yours.

Similarities and Differences. Don't be misled by superficial similarities or belittle significant differences. Differences must be understood and mastered before the similarities—which Americans and Australians do indeed share—can emerge as a basis for effective relationships.

Culture Shock. Almost everyone who spends any time living abroad experiences some degree of culture shock. Some don't recognize it, frequently because it is mild and/or they arrange to insulate themselves from it. For most it is not serious, and sooner or later it passes. For a while, however, some of the symptoms— irritability, exhaustion, inefficiency at work, hostility toward host nationals, and/or a mild paranoia—can have a negative effect on one's efforts to establish good working and personal relationships with colleagues or acquaintances. (For the most concise and useful book on adapting to living abroad see *Survival Kit for Overseas Living*, which is listed in the references.) Be alert to the effects of culture shock and take measures to deal with them.

For Australians

Self-Presentation. One difference which disrupts communication between Australians and Americans lies in the way they perceive and present themselves. Don't hide your accomplishments or underestimate your strengths. Likewise, inquire after others' achievements and talents. Accept recognition and give it as well; compliment your American friends and associates freely. Finally, take yourself and others seriously.

Order and Harmony.   Even though Americans perceive themselves as being "rugged individualists," in reality they seek order and harmony. Therefore, present your disagreements or criticisms in a low-key manner and accompany them with an expression of respect for the other person's position. Compromise on an issue when you feel comfortable doing so. Try to avoid conflict and be sensitive to the Americans' need for approval. They want you to like them and will often go to considerable effort to win you over. Express your feelings when you feel it is suitable to do so, and do it early on in a relationship. Americans distrust, or at least feel uncomfortable with, people who hold back and disclose little of themselves. Try to be consistent in your mood and behavior and avoid contradicting yourself.

For Americans

There are three major areas in which the principles for establishing good relationships with Australians cluster.

Achievement, Recognition, and Status.   Australians rarely give compliments or recognize achievements or status, so don't expect them to. Symbols of status and achievement should be set aside; replace them—if you feel comfortable in doing so—with a little self-deprecating humor. Appreciate Australians for their individual character, not their status or achievements, and don't compliment them extravagantly when they do something well; a few words will suffice. Avoid trying to do things that will make the Australian like you; it will almost always backfire.

Friendship and Sincerity.   Australians don't like to be patronized or be the object of insincere camaraderie. Say only what you mean, avoiding pretense. Use as few words as possible and speak them casually. If a friendship develops with an Australian, be prepared to make a significant commitment to it. Avoid giving the impression that an acquaintanceship is a friendship.

Conflict and Contradiction. Conversations with Australians don't have to be smooth or patterned. Be ready for jarring, colorful statements and shifts in subject. Cultivate and enjoy your own ability to inject the unexpected. Don't agree to something in order to avoid an argument, and don't feel rejected if an Australian disagrees with you. Be ready to be challenged. Take a definite position, stating it forcefully, briefly, and objectively. But don't feel you must defend yourself endlessly; state your case concisely and move on.

For Australians on the Job

Respect for Authority and Status. Americans often like to think of themselves as resisting authority and in the 1960s and 1970s often sported "Question Authority" bumper stickers on their cars. In comparison to Australians, however, Americans accept authority quite willingly. Title and position are important, and even though the manager or executive may slip quite naturally into a first-name basis with workers and "roll up one's sleeves," make no mistake about who is in charge; informal friendliness can metamorphose into stern directives when the situation calls for decisiveness. Try to conform with the somewhat rigid organizational structure with the myriads of memos, meetings, and top-down decision making. Couch your suggestions or complaints in language that will not cause offense or challenge. Likewise, be decisive and in control with workers you supervise. Expect respect for your position.

Achievement and Accountability. When you meet an American, whether in a business or social setting, the first thing he or she will likely ask about you is "What do you do?" Americans are so concerned (obsessed with) doing that someone half-seriously coined the term "human doing" rather than human being to describe them. While most Americans avoid being braggarts, they will find a way to let you know (or "discover") their achievements—job position, boards they serve on, other titles they have held, even athletic achievements. But they expect the same from you. You can be modest about your achievements, but don't hide or downplay them. The other side of achievement is accountability. Just as you will gain respect for your accomplishments, you are held accountable for your actions. You will be expected to measure up to standards. If you make an error or a wrong decision, you will gain respect by accepting responsibility ("the buck stops here"), although, clearly, not all Americans are willing to do this.

Commitment to the Job.   Because Americans value achievement so highly, they are exceedingly goal-oriented and value hard work, gaining their self-fulfillment most often through their career. Your coworkers will expect you to take yourself and your work seriously. When the pressure mounts, you are expected to "knuckle under" and get the job done. A favorite saying among Americans is, "When the going gets tough, the tough get going." You will earn prestige and respect by working hard to meet deadlines.

Remember, Americans make a clear distinction between their work and social life. Although they may "party hearty" with coworkers on occasion, they generally do so with peers, not with those in positions above or below them. You will be tempted to cajole Americans to "lighten up." Have a go at it, but proceed with caution.

For Americans on the Job

Personal Relations.   Officiousness is an occupational hazard for anyone who supervises others. Australians are especially sensitive to it and like to puncture it whenever they encounter it—including in an American office setting. They also expect themselves to be brought down a few pegs if they become overbearing. Directness and informality are the keys to dealing with Australians. Don't let status, position, a heavy workload, technical jargon, or superficial chitchat become barriers to the development of a direct, informal relationship. Like people from many other cultures (Latin Americans, for example), Australians don't separate work and play as sharply as Americans do. Complement your task orientation with a sincere interest in your staff, and attend to the quality of relationships.

Participative Management. Deal with Australians as collaborators. Avoid issuing orders. Negotiate instead, and come to mutually agreeable conclusions. Be easily accessible and approach Australians informally. Don't expect deference. Australians working for you will consider themselves your equal and should be treated as such. When criticism is called for, don't beat around the bush. State it clearly and objectively without making it a personal attack. In discussing business matters don't spend a lot of time on peripheral details, fine points of interpretation, or splitting hairs. If complex technologies or processes need to be explained, avoid a patronizing tone.

Organizational Structure. Australians are used to more loosely organized work situations than are Americans. Try to avoid rigidity in applying rules and regulations to them—and the fewer the better. Australians are more sensitive to unwritten than to formal rules of conduct. Make sure your standards of performance are reasonable, clear, and acceptable to the Australians and keep them to a minimum. Don't expect Australians to be willing to work under the pressures that Americans are willing to accept. While the pace at which Australians are most productive may be slightly faster than what they are used to at home, the relatively extreme pace and pressure of the American workplace may be too much for them and may produce irritation and inefficiency. Job assignments, workloads, and schedule should take account of the preferences and priorities of the Australians and should be negotiated with them.

Labor Relations.   Try to temper your approach in communicating management's position in labor-sensitive negotiations. Make realistic plans that are culturally appropriate—short profit cycles may not be realistic. Avoid direct use of power and above all stay flexible.

Most important, make "a fair go for all" your ruling principle when dealing with Australians. And, by all means, party with your Australian coworkers. Loosen up, let go a bit, but don't make any appointments for early the next morning!

5

A Shared Future

Both the United States and Australia are relatively young nations, still in the process of clarifying exactly who they are. In respect to each other their roles are changing—from being benefactor and dependent to being partners.

The United States in particular is dealing with a new world reality. Since 1960, for example, the U.S. share of "gross world product" has decreased from over a third to about one-fifth. The American philosophy of self-fulfillment and self-reliance is no longer compelling. Self-reliance, though still desired, is no longer possible with the emergence of Japan as an economic power and with the advent of the new Europe; functional interdependence is critical. Like Australians, Americans are searching and debating. They are in need of compelling ideas suitable to the modern age and a new integrating and motivating sense of purpose and direction. As yet, they have not found their center, but perhaps the changes taking place in Eastern Europe will provide the necessary stimulus.

For Australia, the goal is not to become more like the United States despite the dependence Australians have on its products and techniques. Clearly, much of what the U.S. has to offer the world, and Australia in particular, is attractive, so much so that the distinguished Australian architect, Robin Boyd, has coined the term "Austerican" to describe his people's susceptibility to the manifestations of American culture. On the other hand, Australians are critical of the extremes of American materialism. Furthermore, they are determined to be independent, self-motivated, and as self-sufficient as possible.

Australians don't seem very concerned with their origins as a nation, sensing little continuity of traditions over the generations. There is no powerful idea of "where we've been as a nation," yet exuberant optimism is shared by native-born and foreigner alike. There abides a deep sense of being "the lucky country," a midsize nation of consequence in world affairs, where life is good. They cite (as well might Americans) the incontrovertible evidence of the continual flow of others to their shores as proof.

Nevertheless, despite the desire of both peoples to be distinct and self-assertive, there is a strong bond between these two cultures built on their common history and, to a large degree, their shared experiences of emerging as nations over the same period of time. While there is no doubt which country is preeminent, a partnership is evolving which holds exciting opportunities for both. Contacts will undoubtedly increase during the coming decades. More will be at stake. In addition to military alliances and mutual government agreements, Americans will continue to work in Australia, often in subsidiaries of U.S. companies. Australians will work in the United States on short- and long-term assignments. Finally, increasing numbers of people from both countries will be involved in joint projects in third countries, especially in Asia.

With realistic expectations and sincere efforts to adapt to each other smoothing the way, their shared future looks promising.

References and Other Sources

Clark, Alfred W., and Sue McCabe. "Leadership Beliefs of Australian Managers," *Journal of Applied Psychology* 54, no. 1, Part 1 (February 1970).

Conway, Ronald. *The Great Australian Stupor: An Interpretation of the Australian Way of Life*. Melbourne: Sun Books, 1971.

_____. *Land of the Long Weekend*. Melbourne: Sun Books, 1978.

Crawford, R. M. *Australia*. London: Hutchinson University Library, 1970.

Greenway, John. *Australia: The Last Frontier*. New York: Dodd, Mead and Company, 1972.

Hornadge, Bill. *The Australian Slanguage*. North Ryde NSW: Methuen Australia PTY Ltd., 1986.

Horne, Donald. *The Australian People: Biography of a Nation*. Sydney: Angus & Robertson, 1972.

Kohls, L. Robert. *Survival Kit for Overseas Living: For Americans Planning to Live and Work Abroad*. Yarmouth, ME: Intercultural Press, Inc., 1984.

Learmonth, Nancy. *The Australians: How They Live and Work*. New York: Praeger Publishers, 1973.

McGregor, Craig. *Profile of Australia*. London: Penguin Books, 1968.

Moore, T. Inglis, ed. *The Australia Book*. South Yarra, Victoria: O'Neil Publishers PTY Ltd., 1982.

National Geographic, "Australia: A Bicentennial Down Under" 173 (February 1988).

Renwick, George W. "Research and Evaluation of Cross-Cultural Training Programs Involving Australians and Americans." In-house reports, 1975-1980.

Stewart, Edward C., and Milton J. Bennett. *American Cultural Patterns*. In press. Yarmouth, ME: Intercultural Press, Inc., 1991.

Terrill, Ross. *The Australians*. New York: Simon and Schuster, 1987.

Walsh, Maximillian. *Poor Little Rich Country: The Path to the Eighties*. London: Penguin Books, 1979.

Ward, Russel. *Australia*. Englewood Cliffs, NJ: Prentice-Hall, Inc., 1965.

_____. *Such Was Life: Select Documents in Australian Social History Vol I, 1788-1850*. Arncliffe. NSW: Alternative Publishing Cooperative Ltd., 1978.